QUESTION

Well, what is it all about? What exactly is the matter and
who is to blame, and what's to be done about it anyway.

CWESTIWN

Wel, beth mae'r holl beth amdani? Beth yn union sy'n bod,
a phwy sydd ar fai, a beth sydd i'w wneud beth bynnag.

***

FABLE

There is something pitiful as well as disgusting about
the disorder of the scene of last night's orgy. The fun
of the frolic, the assault and battery, the wild scramble
for the money among the muck, all seemed to the luckiest
participants in it as rather glorious while it lasted. No
doubt to a few it may seem glorious still – those lucky
few who after the initial remorseful awakening have been
able to steel away from the disordered scene to other and
still unblemished places. But to the deserted commonality,
by whose labours the orgy was made possible, and whose own
share of the fun was precisely nil, the morrow's dawn upon
the waste and ruin is indeed an unpleasant one.

CHWEDL

Mae yna rhywbeth truenus yn ogystal a ffiaidd am yr anrhefn
yn yr olygfa o'r gloddest y noson cynt. Hwyl y rhialtwch,
yr ymosod a churo, y sgrialfa gwyllt am yr arian ymysg y
baw, roedd hyn i gyd yn teimlo i'r cyfranwyr ffortunus
yn ogoneddus tra'r roedd hi yn parhau. Heb os nac onibai,
i rhai, fyddai hi o hyd yn teimlo'n ogoneddus – y rhai
ffortunus a oedd, ar ol y deffro edifarus, yn gallu dianc
o'r olygfa anrhefnus i fannau dilychwyn. Ond i'r Werin
gadawedig, trwy eu hymdrech yr oedd y gloddest yn bosib,
a'u rhan o'r hwyl oedd, yn fanwl, dim, roedd y wawr nesa
dros y dinistr a'r difrod yn wir yn annifyr.

＊

OPTIMISTIC THOUGHT

There is a clean new world awaiting us just round the corner, and it is not likely to be attained by any of the fashionable faiths current to today. The communists and the fascists and the older political parties can only think in political terms.

MYFYRDOD FFYDDIOG

Mae yna fyd newydd glan yn aros yn agos i ni, a dydy hi ddim yn debygol o'i hennill trwy'r ffyddiau ffasiynol cyfredol heddiw. Mae'r Comiwnyddion a'r Ffasgyddion a'r Pleidiau Gwleidyddiol traddodiadol ond yn gallu meddwl yn nhermau gwleidyddiol.

***

DICTUM

What is wrong with the Conservative Party is that it seeks to conserve the wrong things, with the Liberals and the Radicals that they are respectively neither, with the Communists that all Marx and no Morris has made them dull boys, and with all of them that they don't care because they haven't thought …

DYWEDIAD

Beth sy'n bod ar y Blaid Geidwadol, sydd yn dymuno amddiffyn y pethau anghywir, a'r Rhyddfrydwyr a'r Radicalwyr, sydd yn ol eu drefn, yn naill na'r llall, gyda'r Comiwnyddion, bod llond Marx a dim Morris wedi creu bechgyn anneallus, ac efo nhw i gyd, bod dim ots gyda nhw am eu fod heb feddwl …

***

PROPHECY

The danger of proletarianism is near.

RHAGDDYWEDIAD

Mae peryg proletariaeth gerllaw.

***

DECLARATION

No art that is only one man deep is worth much; it should be a thousand men deep. The modernists are only one idea deep at the moment; it is a good idea; but they shouldn't regard the pattern of social life with the grim purposefulness of American police chiefs contemplating a gang clear up.

ARAFIAD

Nid yw celfyddyd un dyn gwerth llawer, mae angen mil o ddynion. Mae gan y Modernyddion ond un syniad ar hyn o bryd; syniad da, ond ni ddylent ystyried patrwm bywyd cymdeithasol gydag agwedd llym pennaethiaid heddlu Americanaidd yn paratoi diddymu criwiau.

***

OBSERVATION

The great majority — the unburied dead — are a perpetual
drag on all progress whatsoever.

A gimcrack civilization crawls like a gigantic slug over
the country, leaving a foul trail of slime behind it.

ARSYLWAD

Y mwyafrif helaeth, y meirw di-gladd, sydd yn arafu o hyd
ar unrhyw ddatblygiad.

Mae'r gwareiddiad ofer yn cropian fel gwlithen anferthol
dros yr wlad, yn gadael llysnafedd ffiaid ar ei hol.

***

FURTHER OBSERVATION

There is a much larger section than you would believe who
regard all beauty as not only silly (there's no money in
it) but as morally suspect (just look at them poets).

ARSYLWAD PELLACH

Mae mwy na fyddech yn credu sydd yn ystyried pob
prydferthwch fel nid yn unig yn ffol (does dim arian ynddi)
ond hefyd yn foesol amheus (shgwlwch ar y beirdd).

***

POLICY

Let him, then, first read the Republic of Plato — it will
be good for him in any event and quite independently of
the special purpose that has caused me to recommend it
— and there learn how the soul of man is wax to take the
impression of its environment. Let a boy grow to manhood
among beautiful sights, harmonious sounds, and just
institutions, and his soul will give forth beauty, harmony,
and justice. Let him grow up in the midst of brutality and
violence, among squalid sights and ugly sounds, and he will
be unjust and violent in his dealings, his soul will give
forth ugliness, and he will not know how to come to terms
with gentleness and beauty.

POLISI

Gadewch iddo ddarllen Gweriniaeth gan Plato — ar wahan i'r
pwrpas penodol sy'n achosi i mi ei hargymell, mae o fudd
iddo — a dysgu sut mae enaid dyn yw cwyr sydd yn adlewyrchu
argraff ei amgylchfyd. Gadewch fachgen dyfu i ddyniolaeth
ymhlith golygfeydd prydferth, cytgord, a sefydliadau teg, ac
fe fydd ei enaid yn rhoi prydferthwch, cytgord a chyfiawnder.
Gad iddo dyfu ymhlith creulondeb a thrais, ymysg golygfeydd
aflan a synau hyll, ac fe fydd yn anghyfiawn a chas yn ei
weithredoedd, fe fydd ei enaid yn rhoi hyllder, ac na fydd
yn deall sut i dderbyn tynerwch a phrydferthwch.

**

BRIEF ESSAY ON CONDUCT

There are people, wherever there is water, upon sea shores
or upon river banks, lying in every attitude of undressed
and inelegant squalor, grilling themselves, for all the
world as if they were steaks, in the sun. There are tents
in meadows and girls in pyjamas dancing beside them to the
strains of the gramophone, while stinking disorderly dumps
of tins, bags, and cartons bear witness to the tide of
invasion for weeks after it has ebbed; there are fat girls
in shorts and youths in gaudy ties and plus-fours.

TRAETHAWD FER AR YMDDYGIAD

Mae yna bobol, ble bynnag mae yna ddwr, ar lannau, neu ger
yr afonydd, yn gorwedd ym mhob ffurf aflan o noethineb ac
annibendod, yn coginio'u hun yn union fel cig, yn yr haul.
Mae yna phebyll mewn caeau a merched mewn gwisg nos yn
dawnsio wrth eu hochrau i sain gramoffon, tra bod pentyrau
sbwriel drewllyd yn cofnodi'r mewnlifiad am wythnosau ar
ol iddynt adael; merched tew mewn trowsus burion a dynion
ifanc mewn teis gorliwgar.

**

REFLECTION

Their aesthetic spirit has been broken on the wheel of
circumstance. They are bound to live and work amidst the
architectural vomit of a soulless age.

MYFYRDOD

Mae eu hysbryd estheteg wedi ei difa ar olwyn amgylchiad.
Maent yn gorfod byw a gweithio ymysg chwd pensaerol oes
dienaid.

**

PLATITUDE

Don't give the brutes bathrooms. They keep coals in the bath.

YSTRADEBEDD

Paid rhoi ystafelloedd ymolchi i'r cythreuliaid. Maent yn
cadw glo yn y bath.

***

BASIC PROPOSITION

The products of the machine are ugly; therefore let us
abandon the machine in favour of handiwork. The towns are
bad; therefore let us live in imitation villages.

GOSODIAD SEILIEDIG

Mae cynhyrchion y peiriant yn hyll; felly gadewch i ni
ymadael y peiriant er lles crefftwaith. Mae'r trefi yn wael,
felly gadewch i ni fyw mewn pentrefi dynwaredig.

***

SECOND PROPOSITION

The products of the machine are ugly; therefore let us
learn to understand the machine, so that we may draw beauty
from it. 'The towns are bad; therefore let us learn how to
make them good.'

AIL OSODIAD

Mae cynhyrchion y peiriant yn hyll, felly gadewch i ni
ddysgu sut i ddeall y peiriant fel medrwn dynnu prydferthwch
ohoni. 'Mae'r trefi'n wael felly gadewch i ni ddysgu sut i'w
wneud nhw'n dda.'

***

PROMISE

Midnight struck some time in the latter part of the last
century, perhaps as late as the nineties, and the day breaks
very slowly — so slowly indeed that the watchers have
wondered if the dawn would ever come. But now there are
bars and streaks of light such as have not been seen for
generations: there are still dark banks of cloud, sullen
and oppressive, but they are shot through and pierced with
the morning light, and are no longer the unbroken masses
that they were.

ADDEWID

Daeth canol nos yn y rhan olaf o'r ganrif diwethaf, efallai
mor hwyr a'r nawdegau ac mae'r dydd yn dod yn araf iawn —
mor araf bod y gwylwyr wedi amau os ddaw'r gwawr o gwbl.
Ond nawr mae yna linellau a stribynau o olau nad oedd i'w
gweld ers genedlaethau; mae o hyd cymylau tywyll di-serch
gormesol, ond mae nhw wedi tyllu gyda golau'r bore, a
bellach nid ymgasgliadau di-dor y gorfennol.

***

CREDO

First utility, then the joyous super utility of artistic creation.

* * *

QUESTION

When will it arrive?

ANSWER

When human nature changes.

SNEER

What makes you think it will change?

DIGNIFIED REJOINDER

It always has.

QUERY

By what method will it be changed?

REPLY

By wanting it to change.

* * *

CREDINIAETH

Defnyddioldeb yn gyntaf, wedyn yr Uwch-ddefnyddioldeb
gorfoleddus o greadigaeth celfyddydol.

* * *

CWESTIWN

Pryd fydd hyn yn cyrraedd?

ATEB

Pryd fyddai natur dynol yn newid.

CRECHWENIAD

Pam wyt ti'n meddwl y bydd hyn yn newid?

GWRTHATEB URDDASOL

Mae hi wedi erioed.

CWESTIWN

Drwy ba ddull y bydd hi'n newid?

ATEB

Trwy eisiau iddynt newid.

* * *

OUTCRY FROM THE BACK OF THE HALL!

All this talk about art is dangerous, it brings the ears so forward that they act as blinkers to the eyes.

BANLLEF O GEFN Y NEUADD!

Mae'r holl glebran am gelfyddyd yn beryglus, mae'n tynnu'r clustiau mor bell ymlaen iddynt guddio'r llygaid.

***

MAXIM

We have seldom mistaken beauty for ugliness in a woman's face if our poets and painters are to be believed, and we are as much at the mercy of the first awakening of spring as ever we were. Beauty is not absolute, but there are certain canons of beauty that are unalterable.

DIHAREB

Rydyn braidd byth wedi camgymryd harddwch am hagrwch mewn gwyneb menyw os goeliwn ein beirdd a phaentwyr, ac rydyn o hyd o dan drugaredd dihuniad y gwanwyn gymaint ag erioed. Nid yw harddwch yn ddiamod, ond mae rhai gysegriadau harddwch sydd yn ddigyfnewid.

***

ADMISSION

We want impregnable strongholds of natural beauty utterly free from any possible act or threat of sacrilegious barbarity for ever – oases of loveliness from which, one day, we may sally forth and reconquer the surrounding wilderness.

CYDNABYDDIAD

Mynnwn gadarnleoedd anorchfygol o brydferthwch naturiol, wedi eu llwyr gwarchod o unrhyw fygythiad posib o halogiad creulon yn dragywydd – gwerddonau hyfryd o le allwn, rhyw ddiwrnod, adael ac orchfygu'r tiroedd gwylltion.

PROPHECY

When the millennium arrives, when battleships are turned
into floating world-cruising universities, perhaps their
guns, as a last act before being spiked will be allowed
to blow to dust the hideous, continuous, and disfiguring
chain of hotels, houses, and huts which by then will have
completely encircled these islands.

RHAGDDYWEDIAD

Pan mae'r mileniwm yn cyrraedd, pan mae'r llongau brwydr
wedi eu droi yn brifysgolion arnofio yn mordeithio'r byd,
effallai gai eu dryllau, fel gweithred olaf, caniatad i
chwythu'n llwch y gwestai, tai a chytiau sy'n tyfu yn
erchyll ac yn barhaol, byddynt erbyn hynny wedi amgylchunu'r
ynysoedd yma yn hollol.

***

A MOTTO FOR THE WALL

I wish I liked the human race;
I wish I liked its silly face;
I wish I thought what frightful fun,
When it is introduced to one.

ARWYDDAIR AR GYFER Y WAL

Dymunwn hoffi dynol ryw;
Dymunwn hoffi eu wyneb dwl;
Dymunwn meddwl am hwyl di ri,
Pan gyflwyner ef i fi.

***

15 of 487 Uncatalogued Boxes

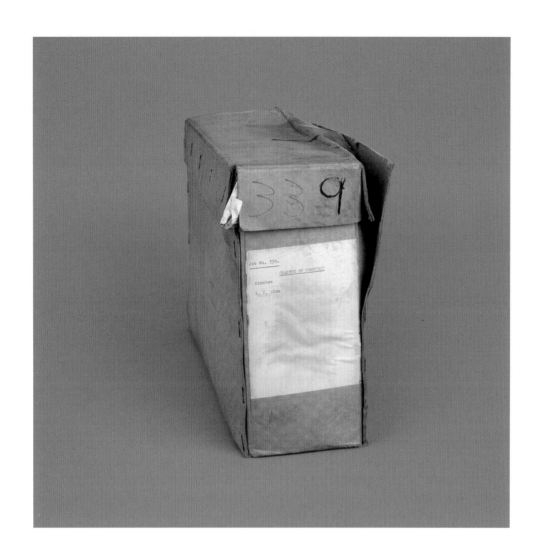

possible to rebuild without money. Owing to the war Berlin
me a poor city. The Federal Government could only help to
extent as West Germany had equally to start again from the
. Without the American credits made available to Berlin
; it would have been impossible to set the economy of the
pital of Germany on its legs again and make it productive.
f of 1954 Berlin had received more than DM 2,074 milliard
source.

construction is one of the most interesting financial experi-
he present day. When the first money arrived no one could
w things would shape, above all whether the various firms
a position to master the arising problems of management
g markets. Thanks to the steadily rising scale of credits
l increasing opportunities to use them, and by careful ad-
· the given situation these problems were ultimately solved.
1,9 milliards out of a total sum of DM 2,074 milliards were
industry, public utilities and transport. The greater part
nd for the special needs of the city. The building pro-
s assured, the increasing volume of orders was financed,
investments were ensured of success by the granting of
redits.

stment was naturally in the first place concentrated on
al groups of greatest importance to the town, those in
ge working capital, e.g. electrical engineering, mechanical
· the steel industry, the precision optical industry, and
industry. Guarantees by the Senate, urgently needed to
er credits, supplemented the either missing or meagre
ters. Especially the smaller and medium-sized firms,
· the clothing and film industries, the latter knit by
th Berlin, could only revive with the help of such
Their great importance can hardly be assessed, as the
with the UFA ateliers in Berlin and the newly founded
mpanies is an economic factor of great cultural con-
at in proportion to the sums involved only trifling losses
d through these investment credits and guarantees does
high morals of the business world and the perspicacity
ible banks and the administration.
ce of five years 230,000 new jobs have resulted from
d of a determined effort to rebuild. What began as an
ogramme and has since been reorganised as a great
gramme helped by very considerable subventions from
proved in the event to be also a psychologically good
tart 50,000, and even now close on 18,000 persons are
· depressing plight of permanent unemployment. They
ection too, for the rebuilding programme not only
·, it sets them to work.

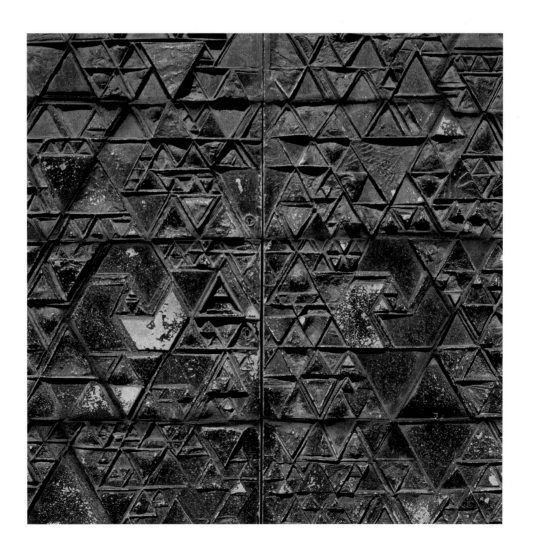

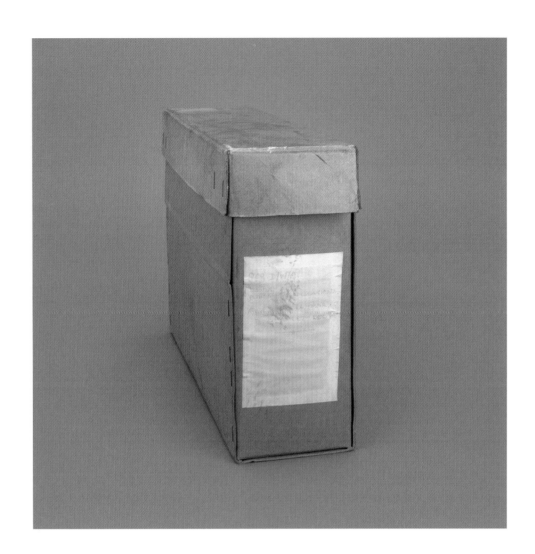

Why contribute to
the spread of ugliness?

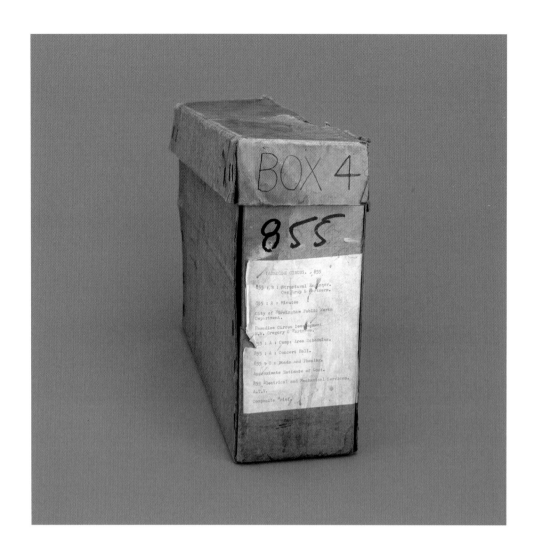

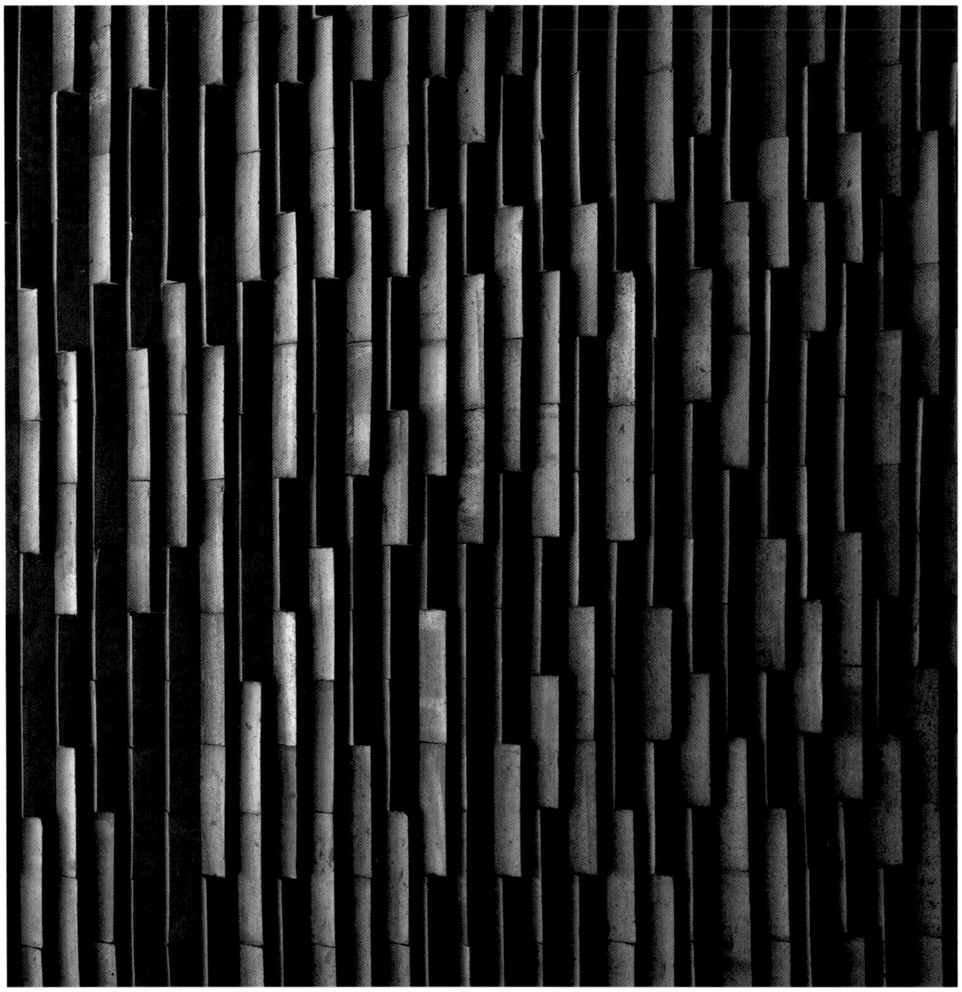

LIBRARIES

RE-VISIT TO U.S.A + Canada
30/11/64 - 11/12/64

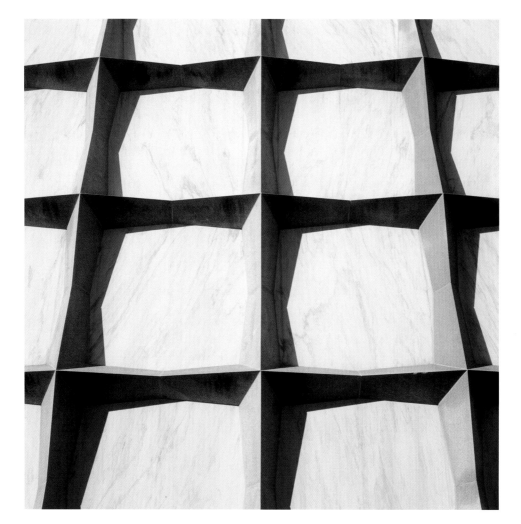

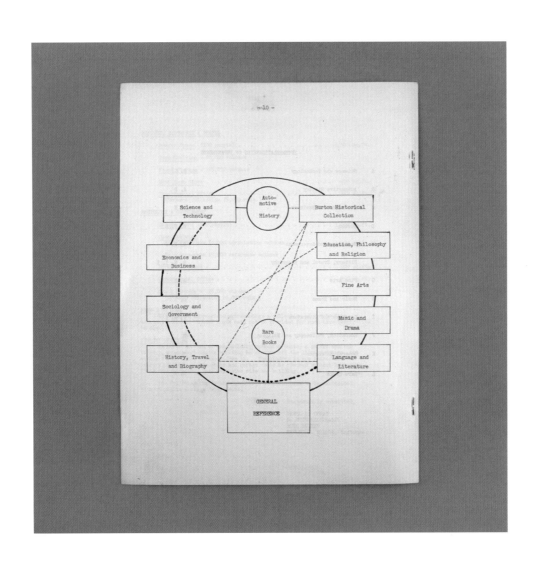

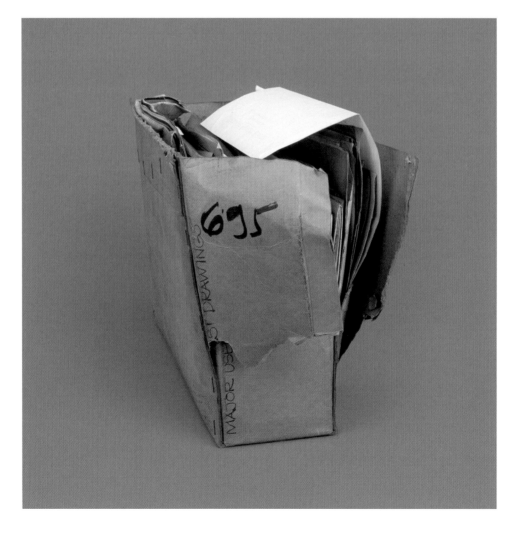

The new will grow out of the old

A GRACIOUS, dignified, well-loved old lady is going into retirement.

Her cloak of green loveliness and her crown of leaves will be donned by a serene young beauty; one who possesses all the virtues of the past, a breath of imagination for the future — and firm determination to resist the villain of the piece, Mr. Bad Planning.

The old "queen" and the new bear the same name — EDGBASTON. And it is a measure of the breath-taking scale of the huge master plan for the new reign of Edgbaston that the transformation will cost millions of pounds and take 40 years to complete.

The rebuilding scheme by the Calthorpe Estates Company, which owns most of residential Edgbaston, is one of the biggest private development projects in the country.

The first 10 years of the plan will cost an estimated £25,000,000.

The story of the birth of Edgbaston and the steady growth of its charm and character is wreathed in the mists of centuries.

Protection

In 1717 the Manor was bought by a rich East India merchant, Sir Richard Gough. Zealously his heirs and successors have striven to prote against invasion able" building.

Now the shield up by the present the estate under ment, Sir Richar Gough-Calthorpe

The need for t of replanning and 1,625 acres, only the heart of Bir twofold:

1. With overcrov ham looking perately for roo population, the areas of the c reviewed in th Development P

2. Most of the Calthorpe Esta torian, built w

SA

★ Each Bargain a F

LADIES

★ Special Offer! LADIES' CREPE WATERPROOFS, in fitted & swagger styles.	**29/6**
LADIES' FULLY LINED WATERPROOF TWEEDS.	**47/6**
LADIES' DOUBLE TEXTURE RAINCOATS. Fully lined. 100 per cent. waterproof.	**79/6**

LADIES' STYLED GABER-

JHDM 339

Berlin Today, issued by Verkehsamt Berlin

Birmingham Chamber of Commerce, original photograph © Birmingham Commercial Films Ltd.

Birmingham Chamber of Commerce

John Piper mosaic, Birmingham Chamber of Commerce

JHDM 2244

Turnese and Aztec, Malkin Johnson tiles

William Mitchell doors, NatWest Building, Birmingham

JHDM Blank 001

JHDM Blank 002

Langley London Ltd., The Tile Centre

JHDM Redacted 001

JHDM Redacted 002

JHDM Redacted 003

JHDM 855 Box 4

Birmingham Central Library, 001

Birmingham Central Library, 002

Birmingham Central Library, 003

JHDM Libraries

Beinecke Rare Book Library postcard, © Alburtus Photography, Yale University, 1964

Beinecke Rare Book Library, New Haven, Connecticut, 001

Beinecke Rare Book Library, New Haven, Connecticut, 002

Beinecke Rare Book Library, New Haven, Connecticut, 003

Beinecke Rare Book Library, New Haven, Connecticut, 004

Detroit Public Library, 001

Proposed enlargement and reorganization of the present main building, Detroit Public Library, 1944

Art and Architecture Building, New Haven, Connecticut, 001

Art and Architecture Building, New Haven, Connecticut, 002

JHDM 776

JHDM 695

JHDM 534

JHDM Calthorpe Estate

Birmingham Post, date unknown

The Botanical Gardens, Birmingham

JHDM 524

Birmingham Post and Mail Print Room, 001

Birmingham Post and Mail Print Room, 002

Birmingham Post and Mail Print Room, 003

Birmingham Post and Mail Print Room, 004

Forward

*I have never been very
certain as to the value of
tangible links with the past.*

– Sir Herbert Manzoni,
Birmingham City
Engineer and Surveyor
1935–1963

The 1960s were the high point of
Birmingham's ambitious post-war
redevelopment programme. After clearing large
tracts of the city's Victorian architecture, the
centre was revolutionised with the completion
of the ring road, the opening of the Bull Ring
shopping centre and the arrival of high-profile
constructions such as the Rotunda and the
Post and Mail building.

At its opening in 1965, the Post and Mail
building was described in an ATV documentary
as 'a proud landmark for the new forward
looking Birmingham'. The scale and ambition of
the building was impressive: the vast advertising
hall, the on-site foundry, the subterranean
machine hall as big as a football pitch. Above
the state of the art printing house stood a
sixteen-storey office block clad in aluminium,
its concrete beams coated with granite and
white marble. At the top of the tower was a
24-hour electric clock flashing out the time and
temperature in six-foot-high figures, a feature so
impossibly modern and exciting that according
to the ATV film, a man living five miles
away chose to check the time each day with
his binoculars rather than look at his watch.

From its futuristic headquarters *The
Birmingham Mail* was a great propagator of
civic optimism, capturing perfectly the typical
second city blend of ambition and insecurity.
Artists' impressions of new grand schemes
regularly occupied the front page. Faceless
people walked across elevated walkways and
empty plazas. Monorails, of course, moved
across the skies. The utopia promised in place
names like Paradise Circus was endlessly re-
imagined and then wiped away again.

The Post and Mail building itself, however, which had taken a decade to plan and build and had been intended to last a hundred years, managed only forty and was demolished in 2005.

There is a melancholy organisation called The Rubble Club, open only to those architects who have lived to see their buildings destroyed. John Madin, architect of the Post and Mail building and many others of Birmingham's post-war redevelopment, must now be considered a leading member, having lived to see three of his notable buildings demolished, with a fourth, Birmingham's Central Library, at the centre of Paradise Circus, soon to follow.

The fate of Madin's Post and Mail building was perhaps even crueller than simple demolition: only the visible parts were demolished, the vast undergound printing house remains. When we speak of the past beneath our feet we tend to imagine fragments and shards. It is then unsettling to find an entire structure intact and entombed. It opens up the idea that all of the city's vanished buildings — the unfashionable, the obsolete, the flawed, the beautiful — were not demolished, but simply archived below ground. Layer upon layer of abandoned structures, patrolled by lonely security guards kicking footballs about their vast echoing spaces.

It's in another underground chamber, beneath the inverted ziggurat of Madin's Central Library, in an area originally intended as a new bus station, that a substantial portion of the architect's actual paper archive is held in 487 cardboard boxes in varying states of repair.

In some ways it seems appropriate that such a key record of Birmingham's post-war development should be underground. The sixties and seventies were Birmingham's subterranean heyday. Whilst the surface of the city was surrendered to cars, pedestrians were channelled above or more often below ground. Few other cities surely could rival the space, care and attention Birmingham lavished upon its underpasses. Whilst a few were straightforward, mosaic lined passages, many more attempted to be destinations in themselves: hidden shopping precincts;

sunken parks set below busy roundabouts complete with water features and public art. Sadly Birmingham's citizens retained a stubborn fondness for surface and sunlight and so the lower tier pleasure grounds became melancholy, lonely, Sunday afternoon type places.

In due course the battered boxes of the Madin archive will be raised up from the depths and carefully moved to the new Library of Birmingham, while the library that currently holds them, the library whose genesis is documented within them, and whose construction heralded the controversial demolition of the old Victorian library, will itself be demolished.

I hope to see in the near future a greater and more beautiful Birmingham and I also wish that I shall be one of those lucky men who will, with care and sympathy, be able to graft our city into the finest in the world.

– John Madin, aged 16, December 1940, in *John Madin: Architect and Planner*, Christopher Madin, 2011

Standing shoulder to shoulder in the bowels of the condemned building, the boxes are an uncomfortable reminder of the optimism of beginnings still awkwardly hanging around at the bitter end.

Archives are not accustomed to the public gaze. Concealment is one of their defining features. From the private archives we accrete during our lives, stuffed in under-stairs cupboards or overhead lofts, to public archives in refrigerated subterranean vaults. Whilst much of the justification for this is to do with protecting the fragile evidence, there is perhaps an element of protecting ourselves too. Archives are the detritus of a life or an organisation, the sediment that has settled, and there's an extent to which, as we push the bulging boxes out of view, we are pleading with some unseen other to make sense of it all.

The boxes of John Madin's archive resemble soldiers returning from some gruelling engagement — dirty, battleworn, some damaged, some broken beyond repair. Like the building that houses them they have been buffeted by time. In the light of the building's fate, their survival in one sense seems counter-intuitive. We talk of firm plans as 'concrete' or 'set in stone', but here such language fails us. We must regard the boxes with a certain knowledge. In Birmingham, cardboard has outlasted concrete. But perhaps this is not so strange. The point of archives is to survive and to outlive that which they document. They are there to mark an absence, to trace a crooked line, in curled notebooks and faded photographs, around the negative space of a life or a place. At the heart of every archive is a void.

What is unsettling about the Madin archive is the way in which it seems to telescope time. Madin's eyes, like those of any architect, were set firmly on the horizon of the future and yet now, just a few years on, the boxes seem to speak of an ancient past. The archive is the repository of the ideas and inspirations behind that brief flickering present sandwiched somewhere between the artists' impressions and the wrecking ball — a key phase in the history of the city, of architecture and of urban planning.

The idea of a city remaining only on paper is both forlorn and mythical. I like the concept of 1960s Birmingham as a kind of Brutalist Atlantis for future historians. I imagine them leafing through the archives, ploughing through the minutes of Birmingham City Council meetings and structural engineers' reports trying to find traces of lost underpasses.

One such lost underpass is Manzoni Gardens, a semi-submerged rest area for Bull Ring shoppers in the heart of a busy traffic island, built in 1962. Named after the groundbreaking City Engineer bent on wiping away all traces of the past, it seems appropriate that his memorial is now buried somewhere beneath the new Bullring shopping centre.

Like Manzoni Gardens, the John Madin archive, reminds us that we do not decide what, if anything might be remembered of us and neither do we decide how, if at all, our lives might be interpreted. We can, though, decide to remember and to interpret. We can make new connections and pathways. We can perhaps choose, as some of our predecessors did not choose, to see the value of tangible links to the past.

Hanging on the wall on the top floor of Madin's Central library are two foundation plaques. One commemorates the opening in 1866 of the late Victorian library. Next to it a plaque commemorates the opening in 1974, by Harold Wilson, of the current library. On a recent visit I found myself thinking again of past buildings buried beneath us. I imagined the two plaques sitting side by side next to a third plaque in the new Library of Birmingham. I wondered how many more might accumulate in my lifetime. Above the plaques was Birmingham's motto 'Forward' and above that a single detail had been taken from the top of the city's coat of arms: an arm swinging a hammer.

Catherine O'Flynn

England and the Octopus, Britain and the Beast
Two channel video

In 1951 the Snowdonia National Park was created, its area established by a definition of 'natural beauty'. This action was part of a larger campaign to protect and promote British landscapes for the nation. Despite being in the National Park's centre, the grey slate waste tips that surround Blaenau Ffestiniog were excluded from the National Park.

Video of areas of Snowdonia National Park, Blaenau Ffestiniog and Portmeirion, scripted with extracts from books that were written or edited by Clough Williams-Ellis, the architect of Portmeirion and a polemicist for the preservation of 'natural beauty'. Williams-Ellis was a prominent advocate for the exclusion of Blaenau Ffestiniog from the National Park.

Sources:

England and the Octopus
First published in 1928 by Geoffrey Bles

Britian and the Beast
First published in 1938 by Readers Union Ltd.

On Trust for the Nation
First Published in 1947 by Paul Elek

Architect Errant
First published in 1971 by Constable and Co. Ltd.

and
The Almost Perfect State by Don Marquis
First published in 1927 by Doubleday, Page and Co.

15 of 487 Uncatalogued Boxes
Medium format slides displayed on three Hasselblad PCP80 slide projectors

487 boxes of archival material that spanned the career of the prominent post-war British architect John Madin were deposited with Birmingham Central Library in 2004. The library, one of Madin's largest and most prestigious projects is due to be demolished in 2013. The archive remains uncatalogued.

Photographs document fifteen of these archive boxes, material that is contained within them, and places that are referenced within the archive. Some of these document buildings designed by Madin's practice, others show buildings and locations which are referenced as informing Madin's work.

This is an edit from a larger series.

Stuart Whipps
Why Contribute to the Spread of Ugliness?

Ikon Gallery, Birmingham
30 November 2011 – 5 February 2012

Curated by Tyler Cann and Jonathan Watkins
Assisted by Jenine McGaughran

Ikon Gallery
1 Oozells Square, Birmingham B1 2HS, UK
Tel. +44 (0) 121 248 0708
Fax. +44 (0) 121 248 0709
www.ikon-gallery.co.uk

Registered charity no. 528892

ISBN 978-1-904864-73-8

Edited by James Langdon and Stuart Whipps
Text by Catherine O'Flynn
Designed by James Langdon
Printed by Die Keure, Belgium

Distributed by
Cornerhouse Publications
70 Oxford Street, Manchester M1 5NH
Tel. +44 (0) 161 200 1503
Fax. +44 (0) 161 200 1504
www.cornerhouse.org

Ikon acknowledges financial assistance from
Arts Council England and Birmingham City Council.

Exhibition supported by Birmingham Library and
Archive Services, Birmingham City University and
Arts Council England.

Ikon Staff
Matt Andrews, Visitor Assistant
Emma Bowen, Learning Coordinator
Tyler Cann, Curator
Matthew Hogan, Gallery Facilities Manager
Victoria Jessop, Project Assistant
Deborah Kermode, Deputy Director
Dimitris Koutoumpas, Visitor Assistant
Mrinal Kundu, Visitor Assistant
Emily Luxford, Marketing and Press Assistant
Chris Maggs, Technical Coordinator
Jenine McGaughran, Exhibitions Assistant
Sarah Oliver, PA/Office Manager
Kate Pennington-Wilson, Visitor Assistant
Jean Phoenix, Finance Manager
Roma Piotrowska, Visitor Assistant
Jen Ridding, Learning Assistant
Pauline Ross, Finance Administrator
Kate Self, Learning Coordinator
Richard Short, Technical and Office Assistant
Rebecca Small, Marketing and Press Manager
Richard Stokes, Visitor Assistant
Pippa Somervell, Ikon Shop Manager
Edward Wakefield, Ikon Shop Assistant
Jonathan Watkins, Director
Jeanette Yarnall, IT/AV Coordinator

Ikon Board
Michael Hibbs
Mark Hodgkins
Glenn Howells (Chair)
Anouk Mishti
Catherine O'Flynn
Stephen Pallister
Sadie Plant
Ann Tonks

The artist would like to thank
Nigel Prince
Helen Legg
Diana Stevenson
John Salim
Uzoma Onyemaechi
Micheal Bewick
Nola James
Brian Morrison
Suzzane Breeze
Denisa Ratulea
Brian Gambles
Ela Myszek
Noni Lewis
Peter James
Jim Ranahan
Merle and Tom Sankey
Jonathan Close
Dr. Alex Buchanan
Peta Murphy Burke
Ruth Claxton
Steve Bulcock
Sean O'Keeffe
Michael Dring

Special thanks to Zara Parekh

Supported by ARTS COUNCIL ENGLAND

Birmingham City Council

REWRITING THE BOOK
THE LIBRARY OF BIRMINGHAM

BIRMINGHAM CITY University